Unless otherwise noted, all scriptures are from the NEW KING JAMES VERSION®. Copyright© 1982 by Thomas Nelson, Inc. Used by permission. All rights reserved.

Scripture quotations marked (NIV) are taken from the Holy Bible, New International Version®, NIV®. Copyright © 1973, 1978, 1984, 2011 by Biblica, Inc.™ Used by permission of Zondervan. All rights reserved worldwide. www.zondervan.com The "NIV" and "New International Version" are trademarks registered in the United States Patent and Trademark Office by Biblica, Inc.™

Scripture quotations marked (NASB) taken from the New American Standard Bible®,
Copyright © 1960, 1962, 1963, 1968, 1971, 1972, 1973,
1975, 1977, 1995 by The Lockman Foundation
Used by permission. www.Lockman.org

Scriptures marked (GNT) are quoted from the Good News Bible © 1994 published by the Bible Societies/HarperCollins Publishers Ltd UK, Good News Bible© American Bible Society 1966, 1971, 1976, 1992. Used with permission.'

Scripture quotations marked (ESV) are from the ESV® Bible (The Holy Bible, English Standard Version®), copyright © 2001 by Crossway, a publishing ministry of Good News Publishers. Used by permission. All rights reserved

Scripture quotations marked (MSG) are taken from THE MESSAGE, copyright © 1993, 2002, 2018 by Eugene H. Peterson. Used by permission of NavPress. All rights reserved. Represented by Tyndale House Publishers, Inc.

Scripture quotations marked (NLT) are taken from the Holy Bible, New Living Translation, copyright ©1996, 2004, 2015 by Tyndale House Foundation. Used by permission of Tyndale House Publishers, Inc., Carol Stream, Illinois 60188. All rights reserved.

Printed in the United States of America

First Printing, 2019

Front Cover Image and Design Layout by Misty Boggs | MSG Books

ISBN 978-0-9827479-5-7

MSGPR LTD CO
1511 S. Chestnut
Lufkin, TX 75901
www.MSGPR.com

THE ULTIMATE THIEF

Who has bewitched you?

Gary & Sheryl,
   Thank you for your friendship
and Godly influence on so many.
I pray you will be encouraged
by the message in this book
and if so, please share it.
May the Lord bless your health,
Sheryl and restore you completely.
         Love you guys

Jeremiah Mdlalose • Robert Flournoy *RL*

www.MSGPR.com
1511 S Chestnut • Lufkin TX 75901

Contents

DEDICATION

This book is dedicated to the faithful christians, past, present and future, that have and will respond to the Kingdom mandate in James 1:27 to care for the Zulu orphans that are the innocent victims of the Aids epidemic in Africa.

JEREMIAH MDLALOSE

Jeremiah Mdlalose was born in a mud hut in Eshowe, Zululand, South Africa in 1962. His mother and father had 8 children, but the first 5 died as infants after the parents had been consulting with local witchdoctors. His father became a Christian at a missionary revival, and from that day forward he rejected the witchdoctors and ancestral worship and started a pastoral ministry. With Jesus as healer, the next three children, including Jeremiah, all lived.

Jeremiah, the sixth of eight children chose to follow his father in teaching and preaching to the Zulu people. They saw many conversions to Christianity.

As a young man, Jeremiah attended the Message of Faith Bible College in South Africa. After receiving a Diploma in Theology (AA Degree) there, he continued his education at Christ for the Nations Institute in Dallas, Texas, where he earned a Practical Theology Diploma.

In 2013, he was awarded an Honorary Doctor of Divinity Degree from Alpha Bible College and Seminary located in Ohio, USA.

Dr. Mdlalose is currently president and founder of Light for Africa Ministries, that concentrates on the training of Christian pastors and planting Christian churches in South Africa. Among other initiatives, his mission has established an orphanage for children who have survived the AIDS epidemic in South Africa. In South Africa, he has also established a teaching center to instruct the Zulu people in learning such trades as farming and sewing.

As it happens, Dr. Mdlalose is one of the trusted pastors who minister to the Zulu Royal Household in South Africa, including the Zulu King, His Majesty Zwelithini Zulu.

K-1827 Gwababa Road
KwaMashu, 4360
Durban, South Africa
www.lightforafrica.org
info@lightforafrica.org

FOREWORD

Rarely does the Western world receive cultural information about the tribal systems within the African nations. Most of us within the Christian community understand the tribal concept only as it relates to denominations, but the tribes of Africa - and some Asian cultures - brand their heritage with inbred traditions that have been passed from one generation to another. These traditions become mores, societal practices and belief systems.

Jeremiah Mdlalose was born into the Zulu Tribe of South Africa. In his book, *The Ultimate Thief*, Mdlalose sets out to explain the tribal culture of the Zulus and their ancient religious practices, that include witchcraft.

Jesus encountered the same practices when he arrived on Earth. His tribal ancestors embraced a culture that included animal sacrifices and religious teachings that were established by man in an effort to appease God. These people were afraid of an unseen God, so instead of pursuing a personal relationship, they depended on a priesthood to lead them in God's ways. Unfortunately, as imperfect men, they misunderstood the message from God and thought that they could find eternal life in their religious Scriptures. Through his teachings, Jesus explained that the messages in the law, the prophets and the Psalms were really about Him. So, in the fullness of time, God came to earth to explain the good news of His kingdom, and from his teachings, Christianity began.

Some of the religious leaders misunderstood His message and once again turned the message from God into a religious system that offered no supernatural power. Mdlalose has sought to expose such teachings by re-introducing the Gospel of the Kingdom of God. This Gospel is a message that offers power and authority in the spirit realm to overcome the kingdom of darkness and produce healings and miracles that come from God. If the supernatural power of God does not work in your life, I must ask the question, "Who has bewitched you?"

Randy Delp Ph.D.
Director, CHRIST FOR THE NATIONS INSTITUTE
Association of Bible Schools
Dallas, Texas

INTRODUCTION

GLOBAL ALERT! One of the biggest humanitarian crises that the world has ever seen is going on right now in South Africa. If you don't live there, you probably don't even know that the HIV AIDS epidemic is happening, much less the magnitude of it. There are presently 7.9 million South Africans, out of 55 million, who are living with AIDS, and 45% of all deaths each year are related to HIV. Since HIV destroys the immune system, most die from TB, flu, pneumonia or hundreds of other diseases. Many are dying from sheer starvation.

As bad as the problem is for the millions of consenting adults, the bigger problem is the three million innocent children that are barely living. Most have lost their parents to AIDS and are homeless. Many are infected with HIV. In the Zulu province, where I was raised, most of the people still live in mud huts with no electricity or sanitation. Unemployment is about 70%, and crime, including rape, murder and sex trade, is rampant. Poverty is staggering.

I am a Christian pastor and teacher and am expected to offer hope to this mass of struggling humanity. I was called by God to take care of these orphans in need, according to James 1:27, but the task is overwhelming. I have built an orphanage for twenty-four children and provide food for about one hundred daily, but this is just a drop in the ocean compared to the need.

I did not choose to be born into this part of the world at this time in history. Was it coincidental or did God choose this mission for me? Did He also choose a divine purpose for me?

If so, has He equipped me for the task? I am just one person; can I really make a difference?

I knew very well the scripture where Jesus said: "**With God all things are possible**" (Matthew 19:26). I knew that Jesus also said in John 10:10 (NKJV) that: "**The thief does not come except to steal, kill and destroy.**" Death and destruction are very apparent in my country, but Jesus also said that He came that we might have "**life more abundantly.**" It was very clear to me that these young and innocent victims were not experiencing abundance in any physical or mental way. Was the thief (Satan) stealing their abundance? How was he doing that? If we don't know, then Satan must be bewitching us. I don't want to give him credit, but that would make him the ultimate thief.

I honestly had to admit that my Christian mission was not producing much help for those in need. Was there something wrong with my theology? Was there a theological crisis going on in my life that I was not able to see? Was there power and provision in God's plan for me to make a real difference? I knew the scripture in 2 Corinthians 12:9 that said <u>in His strength, my weakness is made perfect</u>. That had to be true because God said it, but how was it to apply to the call on my life to help these orphans?

There I was at 57 years of age and having to reexamine my theology. Was the good news of the gospel really applicable to life on Earth here and now, and if so, what was my role to be? I literally heard God call me through the scripture. He said, "Jeremiah, '**Call to me, and I will answer you, and show you great and mighty things, which you do not know**'" (Jeremiah 33:3). Obviously, there was much that I needed to know that I did not know about the Gospel of Jesus Christ. I had studied and taught others about the goodness of God for years, but was I teaching all there is to teach? I certainly needed to square what I believed with the reality of the crisis in my country. What I thought I knew certainly seemed to be contrary to what I was beginning to believe. God seemed to be showing me that He has a way or a plan to deal with this massive crisis in my nation by motivating His massive army of believers, who already have the love of God living in them, to become His strike force for good. I have to admit that seemed too simple, even though I knew God could do it.

Why was I a doubting Thomas? Had I, like the Galatians in Chapter 3, been bewitched, and if so, how did that happen? Learning to listen outside my religious box and to rely upon the Lord in me, by the power of the Holy Spirit, set me on a new journey. My first question was about Jesus' promise of abundant life for these children. I was being forced to look for a dimension of the Gospel that I had never appreciated. Should my Christian life begin to focus on more than just getting saved and going to heaven? Could I dare expect, or even hope for, an abundant life here on this earth for those less fortunate than I? The Bible certainly seemed to say so. Did this have something to do with the Kingdom of God? Was that God's plan to help these orphans, and if so, how could I have missed this truth?

I knew Satan was a thief because Jesus called him one, but I never thought that his real place of destruction, corruption and deceit might just be in my mind. Apparently, Satan had affected my thinking in such a way that I had rejected the intimate relationship of the One that is able to produce righteousness in us. Certainly, I did not want to believe that <u>what I did not know</u> about God was a result of listening to Satan's lies. Could it be nothing more nor anything less than my ignorance in opening the door of my mind to allow the ultimate thief to come in and steal my righteous thoughts about God's divine provision, through His Kingdom, and substitute a kingdom of my own making?

That revelation began a process of changing direction in

my thinking, causing me to "**hunger and thirst after righ-teousness**" (Matthew 5:6). Hope set in, and conviction and determination followed. The ensuing journey compelled me to heights and knowledge of Him that I had never known. The entire testimony of my life was now leading me in a direction that was full of faith, hope and thanksgiving. I began to understand that the One who had saved me for eternity was wanting me and my Zulu brethren to have an abundant life here and now – through His Kingdom. Certainly, Jesus is coming back one day to finish the work of His Kingdom, but how does that help my orphans today?

This process of self-examination to find the whole truth, after many years in this ministry, has not been easy. Rethinking what you have been preaching for a long time is virtually impossible. I did not want to admit to myself, and particularly to others, that I had not been preaching the whole Truth. Do I dare ignore what I am seeing now, after I have prayed and asked the Holy Spirit to lead me into the truth? I could not deny it any longer. It was there all along just staring me in the face: (1) these are God's orphans and He can and will move mountains to help them; (2) His heart of love is beating in the hearts of millions of Christians around the world who want what He wants; (3) God's compassion is always accompanied with resources to meet the needs at hand; and (4) His resources are limitless, as He empowers His followers to be His hands and feet and His heart and soul to those in need, here and now. How simple is that?

Like everyone else, I needed to know what my purpose in the Lord was, and finally my preordained part, purpose and calling was becoming loud and clear. I had to stop worrying about my orphans and begin "**equipping of the saints for the work of service, to the building up of the body of Christ**" (Ephesians 4:12, NASB). I was clearly being called to help people find their preordained purpose and calling in life, which is to serve others by the power of the Holy Spirit. That power and knowledge is embedded in the Kingdom of God and as we accept that reality, we will all find our place and purpose for life on Earth now.

For years, I had prayed like Jabez, in 1 Chronicles 4:10, that God would bless the work of my hand, enlarge my territory and keep me from evil. He was certainly doing all that by the revelation of His kingdom plan. The Holy Spirit was blowing my natural mind and then infusing it with a vision of faith, hope and love that I could not contain.

This vision was showing me the great and unsearchable things that I had not known (Jeremiah 33:3). Honest introspection is not easy, but it is certainly vital. I am asking you to follow along with me as I seek mind-altering and liberating truth to find the most magnificent revelation of "**this mystery among the Gentiles: which is Christ in you, the hope of glory**" (Colossians 1:27).

As you follow my story, you will see that it parallels with the inquiry and testimony of my friend and Brother in the Lord, Bob Flournoy from Texas. We found ourselves on the Emmaus Road (Luke 24) about twenty years ago and have developed a common bond that transcends our territorial boundaries. After you read my story and his "American Perspective," you will see the Providence of God and His Kingdom at work today.

Chapter One
ZULU HISTORY

Divine providence determined that I would be born and raised in a dark and mystical area of South Africa known as Zululand. It is a nation state with approximately twelve million people that lies on the east coast of Africa adjoining the Indian Ocean, and it covers about 36,000 square miles.

The Zulu people are probably the best known of the African people. Their military exploits led to the rise of a kingdom that was feared for a long time over much of the African continent.

The Zulus are descendants of the Nguni-speaking people. Their history can be traced back to the 14th century, but the time most people recognize came in the 19th century, when a young Zulu prince named Shaka came on the scene and welded most of the indigenous tribes into the powerful Zulu Kingdom. King Shaka ruled from about 1816 to 1828, when he was assassinated by his brothers. During his reign, Shaka recruited young men from all over the kingdom and trained them to be a fighting force like never seen before on the continent.

Within twelve years he had forged one of the mightiest empires that Africa had ever known. During the late 1800's, however, British troops conquered the Zulu territory and divided it among thirteen chieftains. The Zulus never regained their independence from that time forward. Throughout the mid 1900's, they were dominated by different white governments, first the British and later, the Afrikaner. The Zulu attempted to regain a measure of political autonomy, both before South Africa's first democratic election in 1994 and from the subsequent period to the present, but they have been unsuccessful.

Today, South Africa is divided into nine provinces, with Zululand being the largest. It is now called KwaZulu Natal. Its present King is Zwelithini Zulu, the twelfth in succession to King Shaka Zulu. His Majesty King Zwelithini Zulu is considered a great and benevolent leader, one who does not hesitate to say "I am the King of the Zulus, but my King is Jesus Christ."

Chapter Two
ZULU RELIGION

Among the Zulu, the religious belief in ancestral spirits (veneration of the dead) has always been strong. They recognize the existence of a supreme being, but he is far removed from the lives of the people. The Zulu people believe the spirits of the dead mediate between the supreme being and the people on earth.

After the elderly die, people are believed to be sacred and are always respected. Getting old is seen as a blessing. After death, the people continue to honor and seek the blessing and intervention of these ancestral spirits. Offerings and sacrifices are made to the ancestors for protection, good health and happiness. According to their religious belief, ancestral spirits come back to the world in the form of dreams, illnesses and sometimes snakes.

The Zulu also believe in the use of magic. Anything beyond their understanding, such as bad luck and illness, is considered to be sent by an angry spirit, considered to be a generational curse. When this happens, the help of a diviner (soothsayer) is sought. He or she will communicate with the ancestors or may use natural herbs and prayers to get rid of the problem. Even from the time of the aboriginal people, most tribal leaders have consulted medicine men or shaman. The medicine men who knew King Shaka Zulu sanctioned and promoted his despotic rule.

Many Zulus converted to Christianity under colonialism, and many more have certainly been converted by modern-day evangelism. In reality, South Africa is considered to be a

Christian nation. However, ancestral worship has far from disappeared, creating a paradigm that denies the power of God by emphasizing the power of evil spirits. This commingling of belief makes Christianity impotent to affect the culture, and it is largely responsible for the AIDS epidemic, which has killed about five million South Africans.

About 20% of the families have been affected, leaving millions of orphans to fend for themselves. Without a family, they are at the mercy of the elements and corrupt criminals engaged in sex trafficking and slavery. One out of three South African women are in danger of being raped. The infant mortality rate is 34.2 per thousand compared to 5.9 per thousand in the United States. The living conditions in the country are harsh throughout, and thus their life expectancy is only about 57 years (20 years less than that in the United States).

Poverty certainly contributes to the crime and disease. Today, the unemployment rate in the rural area is approximately 70%, and it is up to 40% in the urban areas.

Chapter Three
WITCHCRAFT

Witchcraft is alive and well among the Zulus. It continues to have great influence on the African culture. In Tanzania, for example, 93% of the people say they believe in witchcraft. Over 75,000 have registered as witchdoctors. So, their influence is pervasive, and it is not just about medicine.

Satan's scheme is certainly obvious in South Africa, where I live. He openly uses witchdoctors to pervert the truth. They are recognized and accepted by many as offering help and hope. These ministers of darkness regularly consult with the elect. Even some born-again Christians are deceived by them. Satan's influence through witchcraft is worldwide. In Europe and America, this practice just comes dressed differently, usually masquerading as a minister of righteousness or of good. Witchcraft is an evil tactic that is site and time specific for the individual believer.

For Christian believers, our only response is to appropriate the character and power of the Lord, that is resident in us, through His Kingdom as revealed by the Holy Spirit. We should start by taking a word of advice from the Apostle Paul, who reprimanded the Galatians in Chapter 3, verses 1-3, when he said, **"Oh foolish Galatians, who has bewitched you? You were born again by the Spirit but are you going to now live by the flesh?"**

Witchcraft was the only religion that my parents knew. When each one of their first five children was born, it became sick. My parents consulted the witchdoctors but were told that it was a generational curse, and that they should pray to break that curse. It never happened, and all five children died.

Missionaries from the United States were holding a tent crusade nearby and my father decided to go, but his motive was not to know about Jesus or to get saved. He was more interested in women. He was told that the women on the praise and worship team were beautiful. Since many people in the Zulu culture practice polygamy, my father was hoping he would find a beautiful woman as a second wife.

While he was in the tent listening to the praise and worship team and the preaching, someone brought in a woman bitten by a deadly snake. There were no hospitals nearby, so the only thing for those missionaries to do was to exercise their faith in God and pray for her. My father was sitting there skeptical, saying "I want to see if their Jesus can heal this woman that was bitten by a Mamba snake." The missionaries prayed and that woman was healed. My father saw that miracle with his own eyes, and he was convinced to accept Jesus as his Lord. He did not get a second wife, but he did get a new life.

After my father was born again in 1957, he developed a great relationship with missionaries from the United States, including Dr. James and Corriene Hilton from Dallas, Texas, and George and Debbie Smith from Danville, Kentucky. They were some of those who became great friends and mentors and were instrumental in my spiritual growth and maturity. They started a Bible School where George Smith was the administrator and teacher and Dr. Hilton, the president.

I therefore salute the work that has been done by God's people from the United States of America. Had it not been for the support of those churches and from the Hilton and Smith families, I would not be where I am today.

From that humble beginning, God lifted me up and opened doors for me to further my studies at Christ for the Nations Institute in Dallas, Texas, in 1990. Today, I am also one of the trusted pastors to the Zulu Royal Household. God has given me favor to be able to stand before great leaders of the country to tell them about His love, His great plan and provision for His people.

Chapter Four
MIRACLES

After my father became a Christian, he constantly worked with the missionaries that came to our country and was later ordained to be a pastor who evangelized in the remote areas of our nation.

Many souls came to know Christ and were baptized. Once, while my father was baptizing some new converts in the river Umlalazi, a crocodile swam up to him and opened its mouth to take him under. At that moment, the heavens opened up and the glory of God shown on them as it did when Jesus was baptized in the river Jordan. The crocodile just disappeared, and the event shocked everyone.

My father continued to preach and baptize in that river with authority and without fear. God had given him a testimony. He had been able to shut the mouth of the crocodile just as God's Angel had done to the lion in Daniel's time. Many miracles followed my father. My father was always faithful to declare that it was the power of God. As the Bible promised, "**these signs will follow those who believe**" (Mark 16:17).

This miracle story about the baptism began to spread by word of mouth throughout the region, eventually to all of Zululand. Recently, a distant cousin of mine told me that he had heard a bushman telling the story of the man who was preaching and the crocodile miraculously disappeared. This story of God's miracle is still impacting lives.

There was a particular miracle that also happened to my mother. Shortly after my father had been saved, she became so sick that my family said to my father, "The only way that she can get healed from the illness is for the ancestral spirits to enter into her body, and for her to become a witchdoctor."

My father stood on his faith in Jesus Christ and did not allow his wife to become a witchdoctor, for that would have meant that she would have to practice ancestral worship. He gathered the family and told them that he would not allow it. "If she dies, she dies," he said. But she lived, and God gave her a great testimony.

My mother told me that, when she was on her death bed, she saw herself leaving her body and was transported to heaven. There were people wearing beautiful robes and welcoming her with a powerful song singing "Come and find rest." But she came back to her body and immediately asked the people surrounding her to sing that song with her.

After that, my mother would boldly testify that heaven is real and a place for eternity prepared by God for His sons and daughters.

I also experienced many miracles in my life as a young Christian. Once, when I was driving a car for a missionary, I had an experience that taught me to have faith in all circumstances. Pastor George Smith was teaching me how to drive on one of the township roads in the village of Kwamashu, about twelve kilometers north of Durban, South Africa.

This was a crime-ridden area. All of a sudden, children came out of a school nearby and began stoning the cars on the street. But, in the midst of the violence, a young man in a school uniform came out and told me to get the white man out of there.

I was frightened and shivering. I tried to put the car in first gear, but it went to neutral and would not move. Paralyzed with fear, I had this horrific image of a foreign white man in a black neighborhood, being stoned to death. But the young man who had appeared out of the crowd began to push the other angry students away from the car, paving a way for us to drive out.

Pastor Smith said, "Jeremiah, put it in first gear and drive out slowly until the mob is behind us." I put the car in drive and we got away from there.

As we departed, I looked back, but that young man had simply disappeared. To this day, I believe that young man was an angel sent by God for our protection. George Smith had come to South Africa to preach the gospel of Jesus Christ, and God was making a way for him where there seemed to be none. Had it not been for God, I am sure that we would not be alive today.

Once, in the middle of the night, I saw a flashing light through the front door of my house. Half asleep, I shouted, "Go away," thinking it was robbers and I would scare them off. They replied, "Open the door, we are coming for you. If you do not open it, we will kick this door down," which they did.

Two men came in wearing masks. One placed a 9mm gun to my forehead. Initially, I was petrified and immobilized, thinking my life was over. I was very frightened, but suddenly I felt the power of the Holy Spirit come upon me, and the fear of dying just went away.

Two scriptures entered my mind. One was "For me to live is Christ and to die is gain," and the other scripture was "To be absent from the body is to be present with the Lord." I asked the men what they wanted; however, they did not answer. I waited for what seemed an eternity, expecting to be shot at any moment.

When God gave me the courage to open my eyes, I saw the two men fighting to get out of the broken door. To this day I don't know what they saw, but I do believe that God showed them something that made them run as if someone were chasing them. What had been fear in me had become fear in them. The same God that had closed the mouth of the lion so that it would not eat Daniel and had removed the crocodile that had wanted to eat my father is the very same God that was protecting me. God's glory had saved me again!

On another occasion, I was the victim of torture by "necklacing." That is when a crowd takes a car tire, fills it with gasoline, put it on the victim's neck and sets it afire. It takes only a few minutes for a person to die.

One day, when I was driving a car with my family and some bible college students, a mob came out from nowhere and surrounded the car.

They got us out of the car and took my keys. Within seconds they had a tire around my neck. Again, an unknown man appeared out of the mob and started to shout, "What are you doing? Don't you know this is a man of God?"

Immediately they removed the tire from around my neck, gave me my keys back, and asked me to pray for them. I took the keys and ran toward the car. I told them I would pray for them later. I ran as fast as I could. If that man had appeared thirty seconds later, I would not be here. God is able to keep all that are committed to Him. Thank you, Lord.

Another interesting testimony I will share with you is that of an encounter I had with a woman witchdoctor. One day, I hailed a taxi that was going from Durban to KwaMashu. When I got in, there was only one seat left, a circumstance that forced me to sit next to her. You could easily identify her by the skins around her body and the goat bile on her head, but most importantly, the beading around her ankles and a cow tail hanging from her waist.

I wanted to jump out and take the next taxi, but the Holy Spirit said to me, "This is an opportunity to preach Christ to those who do not know Him."

The taxi was playing gospel music on the radio and the lady witchdoctor was singing along. I asked her, "Mah, do you like gospel music?" She said yes. I asked her how she became a witchdoctor and if she liked it.

She replied, saying no, she did not like it and had never intended or desired to be a witchdoctor, but familiar spirits had come into her body. If she refused, she was going to die.

That point opened an opportunity for me to share with her the story of how my own mother got saved. The truth is that witchdoctors are not witchdoctors because they want to be witchdoctors. They are witchdoctors because of fear created by evil spirits.

I told her how my mother got sick and listened to that same spirit that said she had to become a witchdoctor to get healed. I told her that if she would give me her address and allow me to come to her house, I was certain that the Jesus that saved my mother could also save her. She agreed and gave me her address.

The following week the bible school students and I fasted and prayed, and then I went to her house, trusting God. Sure enough, the witchdoctor got saved. Then I told her that she needed to destroy any dress, beads or other demonic items that tied her to the nature of the evil spirits. Everything pertaining to her being a witchdoctor was burned, and she was set free.

This is proof that the gospel message is able to bring deliverance, even to the witchdoctors, out of the world of darkness.

It is hard for me to recall all the amazing things that God has done for me, but I will share this one other testimony that shook the core of my soul.

Two men came looking for me at my mother's house around 8:30 at night. One told me that he was getting married. He said they were referred to me by my cousin because I'm a licensed marriage officer. So, I sat down with them.

As a marriage officer and a community leader, it was not strange for me to meet people that I had never met before, especially for those requesting my assistance.

While we were talking about the logistics of time and venue, the two men stood up and pulled out guns. Before I could even say a word, they opened fire. My elderly mother jumped in front of me to shield her son from a hail of bullets that cost her own life. I fell on the ground and passed out.

When I opened my eyes, I saw my mother and brother lying brutally murdered on the floor. In that moment, I thought I also died and God was showing me my family. I sat up and looked at my tee shirt, which had two bullet holes in it, but when I lifted it up there were no holes in my body. I was shaken and confused when I realized I was alive.

It was a tragedy that has haunted me for my entire life. Why was I saved? To this day, those men have never been captured. God obviously has a purpose for my life.

Chapter Five
WHO HAS BEWITCHED YOU?

After my father became a Christian, he never consulted the witchdoctors again. In fact, he preached against their authority and power.

It was obvious that Christianity and witchcraft were not compatible. Together, we studied and learned the Word of God and found that Jesus Christ is our mediator with the Father in Heaven and He has given authority to us over all evil spirits.

After I accepted Jesus Christ as my Savior, I remember having to contend for my faith because most people I knew continued to believe in witchcraft. They often consulted witchdoctors in matters of importance, not just sickness and disease.

Clearly, witchcraft was the religious dogma of the kingdom of darkness. It was and is the promotion of pure evil. How was it possible for me to submit to the Kingdom of Light and the kingdom of darkness at the same time?

I knew, according to James 3:12 (KJV), that fresh water and bitter water could not come from the same fountain and that a fig tree could not produce olives nor a grapevine produce figs. So, what was wrong with this picture?

People cannot trust God as creator and provider of life and at the same time consult mediums from the underworld of darkness.

I was beginning to see that the scheme of the enemy was to get man to accept an insufficient gospel. Paul's warning to the Galatian church was direct and to the point. He called them "foolish Galatians" in chapter three, verse one and asked them, **"Who has bewitched you, such that you would not believe the truth?"**

I remembered Romans 3:4, where Paul said; **"Let God be true, though every man a liar."** When I accepted Jesus Christ, I began to know Him as the way, the truth and the life (John 14:6). Any teaching that is a distortion of the Truth is evil and destructive to our Christian faith, which is an unwavering confidence in God's word, which is, from the beginning of time, absolute.

We must give an uncompromising allegiance to His Word, for it will never fail (Luke 1:37). In Isaiah 55:11 (KJV), God said, **"So shall my Word be that goes forth from my mouth; it shall not return to Me void, But it shall accomplish what I please, and it shall prosper in the thing for which I sent it."**

In God's time, He sent His Son to this earth that we might know the Truth (John 1:14). But when we dilute the Truth with anything, it **"leavens the whole loaf"** (Galatians 5:9). I had to realize that we are the foolish Zulus that have been bewitched to think that we can walk in the spirit and obey the flesh at the same time.

God's plan is for us to accept the fact that Jesus is **"the Way, the Truth, and the Life"** (John 14:6). If we refuse, ignore, deny or substitute anything or anybody else for God's plan, we are being bewitched and we cannot be the beneficiary of God's power, promises and provision.

We need to understand how witchcraft works. When we think of witchcraft we usually think of African witchdoctors, but actually witchcraft takes many forms.

One of witchcraft's synonyms is "sorcery," which Webster defines as "the use of power gained from the assistance or control of evil spirits [emphasis added] especially for divining."

The Collins English Dictionary says that "sorcery" is the

art or practice, or spell that seeks to harness the occult or evil spirits in order to produce preternatural effects in the world."

"Preternatural" means beyond what is normal or natural (beyond nature). We must acknowledge that it is evil. It is certainly sin because it denies the adequacy of God's power to meet life's difficult situations.

I began to realize that witchcraft is Satan's way of opposing God and His power toward us.

It is simply a diversion from the truth. Anything that substitutes for reliance on faith in God or a belief in some other source of power to live life abundantly is witchcraft.

It operates by offering reliance on a myriad of things, including man's own knowledge of good and evil, apart from God; man's own attempt at self-preservation; any other religion; ancestors; soothsayers; riches; polytheism; Jewish mysticism; or a thousand other diversions.

Reliance on these things is the same as black magic. Whatever works on man to turn him away from reliance on the power of God is the real intention of the enemy. He has a universal plan that works in every individual life, family, community, and nation, and on every continent. Witchcraft dresses up in familiar attire and offers its services to any who will dare seek anything, from any source, other than the Kingdom of God.

God's plan is to make us sufficient ministers of righteousness in His sufficiency. He has called me to preach His Word with boldness and expect to see signs and wonders follow, but He has also directed me to teach His people and disciple the nations in His ways.

His ways promote and provide abundant living. The Chinese proverb that says "Give a man a fish and he will eat for a day but teach him to fish and he will eat for a lifetime" states a righteous principle.

God's ways are practical and realistic that lead people in paths of righteousness. His ways are not just a list of religious platitudes but are life-giving concepts that work for the good of all.

Chapter Six
QUEST

It is painful and sad for me to watch my fellow Zulus, full of pride, dying of AIDS and other diseases. So many families have been destroyed, leaving an epidemic of orphans. Massive unemployment, rampant crime, and extreme poverty compound the devastation, with no end in sight.

I and my American friends have done what we can by building an orphanage and teaching my people how to farm and start small businesses so that they can become self-sufficient, but the magnitude of the problem is simply overwhelming.

I know that God wants better for my people than just a mere existence, without hope. I have read and quoted what Jesus said in John 10:10 many times. "**The thief does not come except to steal, kill and destroy. I have come that they may have _life, and that they may have it more abundantly_**" (my emphasis).

The first part is happening, but why not the rest of that scripture? Why is the abundant life not available to the Zulu orphans? We pray and we pray, but it is as though heaven has shut up against us.

We feebly seek the hand of the Lord and His provision, but nothing changes. Our Zulu King is a wonderful Christian man who loves his people, and even though he is extremely benevolent, it is impossible for him to meet even the most basic needs of his people.

I try to minister to their needs in every way that I can, but it is simply not enough. There is no doubt that Jesus is the way, the truth and the life, so I wondered if there was sin in my life that was hindering an answer. Is there something about God that has escaped me? I had to honestly address the problem before I could seek the solution.

At the very outset of my quest for an answer, I was confronted with a scripture that seemed to be directed to me personally. It was as if the Lord called my name and spoke through the prophet Jeremiah to me, a Zulu Christian in the 21st century.

In Jeremiah Chapter 29:11 (NIV), He says, **"For I know the plans I have for you," declares the Lord "plans to prosper you and not to harm you, and plans to give you a hope and a future."**

I had to admit that I did not know what that plan was that He had for my life. He was clearly saying to me that He had a plan for me while I am here on this earth. That was encouraging, but it was certainly contrary to all the theology that I had been preaching, which was that God's plan was primarily about heaven and very little about life here and now on earth.

Certainly, God was not intentionally hiding His plan for my life. I was reminded that 2 Timothy 2:15 said that I needed to study to be able to discern the truth. I knew God said to seek and you shall find and knock and it will be opened to you. So, I began studying and seeking and knocking on every scripture and theology that I could find. I was determined to know the truth that would bring relief to my countrymen. There was an answer, and I began to see that it was not what I had been led to believe.

Studying required me to ask questions. So the first question was, should a believer in Jesus Christ expect victory in life as well as victory over death? I heard a resounding "yes" and felt an urgency to reread John 10:10: **"The thief does not come except to steal, kill and destroy. I have come that they may have life, and that they may have it more abundantly."**

38

For the first time, I saw that God is offering us two things here. One is eternal life, and the other is an abundant life while on this earth. Eternal life is settled by the very act of faith in choosing Jesus Christ (justification).

Abundant life on this earth is made possible by the fact that the profession of faith invites the Creator of the universe to take up residence in us. That should insure an abundant life, right?

Apparently not, for it guarantees only the <u>potential</u> for an abundant life. If the same power that raised Christ from the dead, parted the Red Sea, insulated the three Hebrew children from the fire, gave Samson the strength to pull down buildings, gave sight to the blind, and healed the sick is resident in us, how could we doubt that He could take care of our little life problems?

I was beginning to see that abundant life is already in us to provide earthly salvation, but we have to work it out (Phillippians 2:12) by appropriating God's character as our own. Clearly, that is the work of sanctification.

Sanctification is a process that would require me to rely on the Holy Spirit. I knew that He was sent to **"guide you into all truth"** (John 16:13), so I was confident that He was not withholding the answers that I desperately needed. I began praying earnestly in the Spirit and with understanding, as Paul said in 1 Corinthians 14:15.

He sent me back to a scripture that I had read hundreds of times in Matthew 6:33, where He said that I must **"<u>seek first the kingdom of God</u> and His righteousness; and all these things shall be added to you."** Surely, the abundant life that Jesus talked about was part of those "things" that my orphans needed.

If I really believed God's Word, then I had to find out the truth in this scripture. I am ashamed to say that I really did not know what the Kingdom of God was, nor why I should be seeking it before anything else.

Serious consideration of Matthew 6:33 brought up so many questions. What is the Kingdom? Where is the Kingdom? When is the Kingdom? Why the Kingdom? How do I get in on it? Evidently it was something that Satan did not want me to know. Was he using years of religious dogma, through witch-craft, to keep this scripture from becoming a reality in my life?

Then I saw another scripture that really got my attention. Jesus said in Luke 4:43, "**I must preach the kingdom of God to the other cities also, <u>for this purpose I have been sent</u>**." (I underlined that portion of the scripture because it jumped out at me.) If it was His purpose to teach the Kingdom of God, then why had it not seemed important to me?

I had prayed thousands of times as Jesus taught us to pray, for the Kingdom <u>to come on earth</u> as it is in heaven. If Jesus told us that God sent Him to teach us about the Kingdom of God and He said for us to pray for it to come on earth, then surely we could experience it here and now. It felt like the Holy Spirit was about to change my perspective from heaven to earth.

The Holy Spirit then confronted me with Mark 4:10-20 (GNT), where Jesus explained what the Kingdom is like, using parables:

> **[10]When Jesus was alone, some of those who had heard him came to him with the twelve disciples and asked him to explain the parable. [11]"You have been given the secret of the Kingdom of God," Jesus answered. "But the others, who are on the outside, hear all things by means of parables,**
> **[12]so that,**
> **'They may look and look,**
> **yet not see;**

they may listen and listen,
yet not understand.
For if they did, they would turn to God,
and he would forgive them."

[13] Then Jesus asked them, "Don't you understand this parable? How, then, will you ever understand any parable? [14]The sower sows God's message. [15]Some people are like the seeds that fall along the path; as soon as they hear the message, Satan comes and takes it away. [16]Other people are like the seeds that fall on rocky ground. As soon as they hear the message, they receive it gladly. [17]But it does not sink deep into them, and they don't last long. So when trouble or persecution comes because of the message, they give up at once. [18]Other people are like the seeds sown among the thorn bushes. These are the ones who hear the message, [19]but the worries about this life, the love for riches, and all other kinds of desires crowd in and choke the message, and they don't bear fruit. [20]But other people are like seeds sown in good soil. They hear the message, accept it, and bear fruit: some thirty, some sixty, and some one hundred."

This scripture actually told me most of what I needed to know!

First, the Kingdom of God was essential to the life of believers; second, the Word had already declared the Truth to me; third, that when we hear the message of the Kingdom, Satan will come immediately to steal it from our understanding; fourth, that without understanding and acceptance of this message, it is impossible to understand the other teachings of Jesus; fifth, the reality of the Kingdom of God for a believer's life depends upon its reception in his mind – good soil; sixth, if this message about the Kingdom is choked out of our life by Satan, our lives will not bear fruit; seventh, if we hear the message and accept it, we will bear fruit, some thirty, some sixty and some one hundred fold.

When I prayerfully and honestly read these verses in Mark 4, it was as if I had never read them. What made the difference this time? Was the soil of my mind simply ready and prepared for planting and receiving an abundant harvest? Was I ready to embrace the Kingship of Jesus? Would His righteousness be imputed and imparted in a way that my conduct and character would reflect the fruit of the Spirit? Was God's love available to be shared abroad through me?

Obviously, when love becomes the hallmark of our lives, we will exhibit joy, peace, patience, kindness, faithfulness, gentleness and self-control. Individually, we could become a whole person in the likeness of our Savior, and collectively we could change our culture and even the nations!

Could that be true? I was getting a glimpse of the GOOD NEWS, but I still had a lot of questions. How is this liberating truth going to be manifested here and now?

If the Kingdom of God was available to me, it would have to be personal and present. Jesus said several times that the Kingdom of Heaven or the Kingdom of God was near or at hand (Matthew 3:2, Matthew 4:7, Mark 1:15).

That was absolutely correct. It was near and at hand until the time of His death and resurrection, when the Kingdom of Heaven opened up its headquarters on earth, fulfilling the promise of the scriptures.

After the resurrection and before the ascension, Jesus spent forty days with the disciples **"speaking about the Kingdom of God"** (Acts 1:3, ESV). He never again spoke of it being near, because it was here. Phillip preached the same thing in Acts 8:12, and Paul preached the Kingdom of God in Acts 19:8; 20:25; 28:23; and 28:30-31.

So, I was quickly learning that if the Kingdom of Heaven came to earth when Jesus ascended to His throne in Heaven, then the Lamb that was slain before the foundation of the world was the King of kings now.

Chapter Seven
SO MANY QUESTIONS

I still had so many questions. A really big one was about how the Kingdom of God is going to be manifested in the Zulu kingdom.

It was becoming obvious to me that it would not be some physical empire, but transformed lives, one individual at a time. When people submit to Jesus in such a way that God's character and ways are revealed and expressed through them to this world in our generation, they will express the Kingdom of God. My mind was hesitant to this idea, but I believed God's Word and knew what Jesus said in Matthew 19:26, that **"With man this is impossible, but with God all things are possible."**

I did not have to be a rocket scientist to realize that God had sovereignly called me to a seemingly impossible task. He raised me up in the midst of one of the greatest humanitarian crises the world has ever known. The AIDS epidemic has left about 1 million orphans in Zululand alone. Even though it is the largest province in South Africa, it is the poorest, with unemployment around 70%. How could I do James 1:27 and take care of these orphans?

God knew that I could not do this alone! He would have to enlist many more to make a difference. That did not seem likely, but certainly God is living in hundreds of millions of people around the world who could operate out of His supernatural love and power. He could motivate them to do what He has commanded us all to do – not just me.

Isaiah 55:11 says, "**So shall my word be that goeth forth out of my mouth: it shall not return unto me void, but it shall accomplish that which I please, and it shall prosper in the thing where to I sent it.**"

If he sent His Word to me, then I could see how He could send this mandate to enough Christians that we could collectively take care of the Zulu orphans. But I did not see how He was going to motivate the other Christians unless they realized that the Kingdom of God was living in them full of purpose, power and provision.

God is certainly no respecter of persons, so what He had done in me, He could do in others as well. I was motivated! Therefore, they could all be motivated. They simply needed to remember that He came to fulfill His Word and He was going to do it through us, not in our strength but His.

Is the Righteousness, Peace and Joy in the Holy Spirit that is resident within many millions of humans going to be the vehicle for deliverance and salvation for my million orphans? Could my orphans become their million orphans? Was the answer hidden in God's love? Would born-again Christians feel compelled to help? All of a sudden, it no longer appeared to be an impossible task!

Like every Christian I know, we all want to know what God's plan is for us so that we can find our place or assignment in the Lord.

How would we know it for sure, if we found it? Was I even looking for it in the right place? Was I looking for the answer to this question in the Tree of Life or in the Tree of the Knowledge of Good and Evil? Was I confused between God's plan and His purpose? Was I putting the cart before the horse?

As I pondered this, I began to realize that God's plan is simply for us to know Him in an intimate way, and out of His love will flow the direction for our lives. Our purpose will then become clear, along with the conviction to carry it out.

God certainly knows me better than I know myself, so when I submit to His will and His way, I will fulfill His purpose for me and become His grace and provision in the context of service to others.

This is exactly what happened to Simon Barjona. By revelation, he came to know Jesus as the Son of the living God. At that moment, Jesus said, **"God bless you, Simon, son of Jonah! You didn't get that answer out of books or from teachers. My Father in heaven, God himself, let you in on this secret of who I really am. And now I'm going to tell you who you are, really are. You are Peter, a rock. This is the rock on which I will put together my church, a church so expansive with energy that not even the gates of hell will be able to keep it out."**

"And that's not all. You will have complete and free access to God's kingdom, keys to open any and every door: no more barriers between heaven and earth, earth and heaven" (Matthew 16:17-19, MSG). God changed Peter's purpose from fisherman to fisher of men that day.

It is impossible for any of us to find our purpose without first embracing Jesus and His Kingdom plan, which is already within us. The Kingdom of Heaven will surely come to Earth as we find and submit to God's purpose for our existence here and now.

What does the Lord require of us? Micah 6:8 says that He expects us to **"Do justice, love mercy and walk humbly with the Lord."** How can we possibly do that unless He directs our path? We simply cannot do it by leaning on our own understanding (Proverbs 3:5-6).

Matthew 6:33 says that we are to seek the Kingdom of God and His righteousness first and everything else will fall into place. In 1 Corinthians 2:2-5, the Apostle Paul said that all that he wanted was to know the Lord. He was not seeking to know his purpose in the Lord.

Paul, who wrote most of the New Testament, also said that he was not speaking with persuasive speech but in demonstration of the Spirit so that our faith would not rest on human wisdom but on God's power.

Unless the Lord build the house, we build in vain, according to Psalms 127:1. God is the architect for His house, which is the whole world, and we can co-labor with Him only when He gives us our assignment and equips us for our purpose.

God's modus operendi (according to my lawyer friend Bob) is that God will use earthly vessels to invade this Earth now and to fill it with His glory and provision.

Our mind has to be renewed to the truth of God's plan and purpose if we are to be effectual in our Christian witness on Earth. This is where the critical battle is being waged. Jesus warned us that even though He came so that we could have abundant life, there is an enemy whose determined intention is to steal, kill and destroy our purpose in the Lord.

We have to remember that Satan's plan is deception. He is a liar, and a master deceiver, so I was beginning to question if I had been under his spell. Had I been submitting to his religious plan for genocide for the Zulus? Obviously, I needed to pay a lot more attention to the enemy's tactics. God has warned us about listening to the voice of the stranger (devil) in John 10, even before He promised that we could have life more abundantly.

Satan knows full well that we can be led astray by our own will and strength, but the Holy Spirit shows us that the way of escape from our own ways is by God's grace. In 2 Corinthians 12:9, Jesus said, "**My grace is sufficient for you, for my strength is made perfect in weakness**." Jesus told us that we would be better off when He is gone because God was sending the Holy Spirit to be our comforter and helper in time of need. Even the disciples had a hard time grasping the concept of grace as a spiritual law.

The Light of God's Word has to shine on our depravity and expose the fact that "**in me (that is in my flesh) dwelleth no good thing, for to will is present with me, but how to perform that which is good I find not**" (Romans 7:18).

Chapter Eight
A BATTLE FOR THE MIND

In John 17:15, we are told to pray that while we are here, God will keep us from the evil one. That is going to require us to agree with God's Word. Even though we are born again and a new creature, our self-absorbed mind has to be transformed so that we may be conformed to His image.

Why was that such revolutionary thinking for me and much of the Christian world? Could the Kingdom of God be His way of providing for our transformation and abundant life? If our carnal mind, which says, "I want it for myself, my way, and make me important," is not renewed and transformed to the Kingdom truth, we won't have it.

It was becoming obvious to me that as long as we submit to Satan's lies about the Kingdom, we will not receive God's plan, which is **"righteousness, peace, and joy in the Holy Spirit"** (Romans 14:17).

Clearly, our mind can come into conformity with God's absolute Word only when it submits to the Teacher that God sent to insure our ability to get it. However, that Truth is pitted against the fact that we still have the free will to deny it, doubt it, excuse it, refuse it, delay it and confuse it.

This is where the rubber meets the road - where the battle begins and ends. Paul explained it in Romans 7:15-20 when he said that he did not do what he should and did what he should not, because of the sin that was in him. In Romans 8, he points out where the sin problem resides. He said it is in the carnal mind and it is opposed to God, even though the person is born again and destined for eternal life with God.

So that explains why the carnal mind has to be renewed and transformed according to Romans 12:2. When our mind is renewed to the truth, then we will be able to test and approve what God's perfect will is for us. Jesus told us that His will is for us to have an abundant life, but He also told us that we have an enemy that has a plan to steal the knowledge of the promise of that abundant life from us. That enemy remains present with us as long as we are on the earth. Satan is always acting like a roaring lion seeking whose life he may devour. Fortunately for us, the Word tells us in James 4:7 that if we submit ourselves to God and resist the devil, he will flee.

We need to acknowledge that the devil has an evil tactic designed specifically to keep us from submitting ourselves to the One who wants to be the Lord and Master of our life.

This present struggle between life more abundantly and hell on earth rests upon one word: "submission." There are two kingdoms, and we will submit to one or the other. The Word says in Matthew 6:33 that we are to submit or **"seek first the Kingdom of God and His righteousness and all these things shall be added to you."**

Through his lies and evil tactics Satan comes to all of us while here on earth and constantly tries to persuade us that darkness is better than light, that lies are better than truth, and that the Kingdom of God is not real or not for this present age.

Satan's workshop is in my mind. He knows that Jesus came as the light of the world but he also knows that according to John 3:19, man loves darkness more than light. God offers us the Kingdom of light through our submission, but if we reject it, we submit to the kingdom of darkness.

Jesus said **"No one can serve two masters. Either you will hate the one and love the other or you will be devoted to one and despise the other"** (Matthew 6:24, NIV).

The dilemma for us is in deciding which master we will submit to. Since it is Satan's avowed purpose to exalt his throne and kingdom above the Kingdom of God (Isaiah 14:13), we must take him seriously. Our lives will be subdued by one kingdom or the other, one master or the other. Whom we choose determines our destiny.

In Deuteronomy 30:19, God says, "**I call heaven and earth as witness this day against you, that I have set before you life and death, blessing and cursing; therefore choose life, that both you and your descendents shall live.**" He said in the Garden of Eden that there are two trees: The tree of life, representing God and His plan, and the tree of knowledge of good and evil, representing man's carnal nature, which is inherently evil. The choice is simple, but not so easy because we have to decide with our mind. It cannot be a little of this and a little of that.

There can be no shared allegiance. We will play by one of two strategies. One leads to victory and one leads to defeat. We don't choose the strategy or play book, but we choose the master coach.

The greatest battle for life or death is fought at "but choose." Our heart wants to accept God's choice, but the mind does not. The battle is not over until our unregenerated mind accepts the fullness of the Lord for life on earth, not just savior for eternity. Our minds have to be renewed daily for our acceptance of the Lord to be effectual here and now.

Satan's evil plan is not over when we say "I do" to the Lord. Satan knows that, as a born-again Christian, we are still vulnerable in our minds. He is an expert at brainwashing. He focuses on our natural proclivities, such as the "**lust of the flesh, the lust of the eyes and the pride of life**" (1 John 2:16).

Satan knows ours desires and uses them against us so that we will not be an effective adversary to him.

This is truly the most important battle we will ever fight –

it is a spiritual fight to the death – it is where darkness fights the light. God has done all He will do. We now have to make up our own mind to choose what He has already chosen for us. The choices are made in the mind, so it is now up to us to make Godly decisions.

We are challenged by God in Joshua 24:15 to "**choose you this day whom you will serve.**" That was the battle cry of Joshua, who was a great warrior. It would have to become mine as well.

Our mind will go to any lengths to get us to make the wrong choice. Since this is the place for our personal and individual Armageddon, we can win only by agreeing with God.

The scripture in Ephesians 6:12 says "**we do not wrestle against flesh and blood, but against principalities, against powers, against the rulers of darkness of this age, against spiritual hosts of wickedness in the heavenly places.**" If we accept that truth, then we can and must accept the truth in 2 Corinthians 10:4 that "**The weapons we fight with are not the weapons of this world.**" Our spiritual weapons have divine power to demolish strongholds in our mind.

How do we do that? The scripture says that we can do it by "**Casting down imaginations and every high thing that exalteth itself against the knowledge of God, and bringing into captivity every thought to the obedience of Christ**" (2 Corinthians 10:5, KJV). Bringing our thoughts into conformity with God's - That's how!

God has given us the power to bring our mind and thoughts into obedience to His Word. As Christians, we want to be obedient, but the enemy definitely does not want that. The truth is that we can't be obedient unless God motivates us. That is why Paul said in Galatians 2:20 that his whole being had to be crucified in Christ.

He knew that it was Christ in him the hope of glory, and that the life that he was living on this earth, he lived by Christ's life and the faith <u>of</u> the Son of God, who loved him and gave Himself for him.

Paul said that he lived in the flesh by the faith of the Son of God. It was not Paul's faith, but submission to the faith of Jesus that was residing in him. Jesus' faith can move mountains, but not Paul's nor mine.

We find many attributes <u>of</u> God that are resident in us, like the Peace <u>of</u> God that passes all natural understanding (Philippians 4:7) and the love <u>of</u> God that cannot be separated from us, for God is love (1 John 4:8). **"The Joy <u>of</u> the Lord is my strength"** (Nehemiah 8:10).

"The fruit <u>of</u> the Spirit is love, joy, peace, long-suffering, kindness, goodness, faithfulness, gentleness, and self-control. Against such, there is no law" (Galatians 5:22-23). When God, who is Love, is resident in us, we are partakers of all the other traits of His nature.

The Holy Spirit is the catalyst that ignites a personal identification with these attributes, and when that enlightenment occurs, those traits will collectively order our lives, our families and communities by and through a new kingdom – the Kingdom of Love.

I was finally getting it. God wants us to become a kingdom of kings and priests (Exodus 19:6 and Rev. 1:6), operating by and through His love to rule and reign with Him on the Earth now.

That is when He is King of kings. First Peter 2:9 (KJV) declares that we **"are a chosen people, a royal priesthood, a holy nation, God's special possession, that you may declare the praises of him who calls you out of darkness into his wonderful light."** And where are we going to experience this? On Earth – not in heaven!

Chapter Nine
THE FRUIT OF THE SPIRIT

How could I appropriate the fruit of the Spirit in Galatians 5 into my life? It was becoming clear that God had to do it in me sovereignly.

Obviously, I just had not appreciated the fact that He had already invaded my life with Himself and an all- consuming love when I was born again.

Did that mean that I could actually experience the Beatitudes in my life? God said in Luke 17:21 that **"the Kingdom of God is within me,"** and Romans 14:17 says that **"the kingdom of God is not eating and drinking but righteousness, and peace, and joy in the Holy Spirit."**

Wow! Apparently, my part in God's plan was just to submit and receive. That seemed too good to be true! Could it be the answer to the plight of the Zulus?

The fruit of the Spirit describes the divine nature of God that begins to reside in each of us when we are born again. We adopt these attitudes as our own by belief, faith and submission through the indwelling power of the Holy Spirit.

These divine characteristic traits are just waiting to get out of our body and influence the world around us. Christians clothed in the divine nature of God, set loose on the world, will establish and be His kingdom.

Love, joy, peace, long-suffering, kindness, goodness, faithfulness, gentleness and self-control become our character.

We cannot and will not manifest these characteristics on our own – even as born-again Christians. It requires submission to the teaching and training of the Holy Spirit to have a renewed mind so we can know and follow the perfect will of God. It is "**Not by might, nor by power, but by My Spirit says the Lord of hosts**" (Zechariah 4:6).

That is an absolute fact, and the sooner believers come to that point of understanding and acceptance, the sooner we will line up with God's perfect plan for us. Even when we agree with that fact, it can be a difficult concept for us to truly embrace. We fight for victory over the enemy by submitting our physical and mental abilities to the Holy Spirit, who equips our character to stand for and with a righteous shield and sword.

I knew the Holy Spirit would have to reveal this to me. Even as a born-again Christian, I did not fully understand that my personal strategy for fighting Satan was not adequate.

Paul said that in God "**we live and move and have our being**" (Acts 17:28). "*Being*" is the operative word. I thought it was my doing or not doing, but not doing was contrary to everything that I had believed about my macho self.

Again, I was beginning to recognize that the stronghold was in my mind. If my mind could change to accept God's plan for me, it would substitute my way of thinking and my attitudes with God's divine nature. Thus, I could actually put on the mind of Christ (1 Corinthians 2:16).

I remembered the scripture in Philippians 2:5 that admonished us to "**let this mind be in you, which was also in Christ Jesus.**" Therefore, it is the fruit of the Spirit that actually changes our character traits to become Jesus' armaments of war to battle the enemy.

That is certainly a different kind of kingdom than the one I grew up in. I really thought that the Kingdom of God would be like the kingdom of the Zulus, but with abundance. How wrong I was!

God simply intends to fill this whole earth with people that are filled with the new paradigm that comes from the love of

58

God and a mind that is conformed to the truth that guides their spirit and actions. We, as sons of the Kingdom, will be the new heaven and the new earth. In John 18:36 Jesus said "**My kingdom is not of this world**," meaning that it is spiritual and not physical, but it manifests itself in the physical here and now. Jesus said to pray that His Kingdom come on Earth and that His will be done on Earth.

It began to make absolute sense to me that His kingdom would come, not as some cataclysmic event or battle, but as just one new believer at a time.

Imagine a new man, expressing the love of God, taking his place and becoming leaven, salt and light, husbands, wives, parents, teachers, soldiers, builders, janitors and kings, all with a free will motivated and led by peace and joy in the Holy Spirit. That was almost too much to take in.

Chapter Ten
THE THIEF COMES TO
STEAL, KILL AND DESTROY

I admit that I was still confused about how Satan comes to steal, kill and destroy. Do we unwittingly become his instruments of destruction? Does he pervert our thinking with tempting thoughts that appeal to the soul (mind, will and emotion)?

Satan began in the Garden when he created doubt about what God said, and thereby began the process of stealing our heritage in the Lord. That is why Jesus called him a thief. If he could get Adam and Eve to doubt God, he can do that to us. He is truly the *ultimate thief.*

When we listen to his tempting thoughts and accept them, we become defeated Christians. Satan is satisfied to just make us double-minded. That is why God warns us that; **"a double- minded man is unstable in all of his ways"** (James 1:8, KJV). **"Let not that man think he will receive anything of the Lord"** (James 1:7, KJV).

Allowed to prevail, doubt becomes denial and then hostile to the truth. Our Zulu society has rejected the truth so long and to such a degree that God has seemingly given us over to a "reprobate" mind (Romans 1:28).

It became clear to me that it is a rejection of God's governmental plan that has led to such destitution in my nation. Satan also has a plan, and that is to convince us that God does not have a plan for our life that we can trust. If he can get our mind to doubt the inerrancy of God's word, it will not be worth trusting. If we don't believe that it is all true, we won't be sure any of it is.

The Kingdom of God is a spiritual concept that manifests in the here and now for those individuals and nations (groups of people) that genuinely believe it. Our carnal mind, and in fact our society, can and does easily accept the gospel of salvation because its benefits are without cost and are an easy option for life eternal.

The gospel of the Kingdom requires more of us. It requires an abiding lifestyle by submission. Abiding in Christ means allowing the Lord and His Word to fill our minds, direct our wills and transform our affections.

The dictionary definition of "abide" is to comply with, observe, follow, hold to, conform to, stick to, stand by, uphold, pay attention to, agree with, consent to, accept, acquiesce in, acknowledge, have respect for, and defer to.

Jesus said "**If you abide in Me and My word abides in you, you can ask what you desire and it shall be done for you**" (John 15:7, NIV). So, if we abide with the Creator of the universe and the Lover of our soul, then we can ask what we will that pertains to <u>life and godliness</u> (2 Peter 1:3) and it shall be done for us.

Submission is really the place of our spiritual battleground. Satan hates our submission to God, so it is more difficult than just believing. Man's unregenerated mind always wants to exalt itself above the throne of God (Isaiah 13:14). We have to accept the fact that we can no longer lean on our own understanding (Proverbs 3:5, 6).

His Word must become a lamp for our feet and a light on our path (Psalms 119:105). We have to humble ourselves under the mighty hand of God that He may exalt us in His time (1 Peter 5:6). Submission is active, not passive. It is a choice that does not occur naturally.

In Galatians 6:7 (KJV), Paul reminded us: "**Be not de-**

ceived; God is not mocked: for whatsoever a man soweth that shall he also reap."

These words should be a warning for anyone seeking to know God and His ways. If we don't heed this admonition, we can find ourselves with the mindset of the Galatians and be just as deceived as they were.

Paul said in Galatians 3:1-3 (KJV), **"O foolish Galatians! Who has bewitched you that you should not obey the truth, before whose eyes Jesus Christ was clearly portrayed among you as crucified? This only I want to learn from you: Did you receive the Spirit by the works of the law, or by the hearing of faith? Are you so foolish? Having begun in the Spirit, are you now made perfect by the law?"**

Many Zulus are born again by the Spirit, but the question remains, will we continue to live double minded lives with part of our mind choosing God and part of it choosing something else?

Settling for only eternal salvation is anathema to God's plan for the born-again child of God. It is completely selfish and irresponsible and takes God's name in vain. He did not sacrifice His son just so that we could go to Heaven when we die. That is not the whole gospel; that is being double minded.

In the Kingdom of God, we occupy. We put on the whole armor of God (Ephesians 6:11-18)

> **"that you may be able to stand against the wiles of the devil. For we do not wrestle against flesh and blood, but against principalities, against powers, against the rulers of the darkness of this age, against spiritual hosts of wickedness in heavenly places. Therefore, take up the whole armor of God that you may be able to withstand in the evil day, and having done all, to stand."**
>
> **"Stand therefore, having girded your waist**

with <u>truth</u>, having put on the breastplate of <u>righteousness</u>, and having shod your feet with the preparation of the <u>gospel of peace</u>, above all, taking the shield of <u>faith</u> with which you will be able to quench all the fiery darts of the wicked one. And take the helmet of <u>salvation</u> and the sword of the Spirit which is the <u>word</u> of God; praying always with all prayer and supplication in the Spirit, being watchful to this end with all perseverance and supplication for all the saints."

This is the way to form the ultimate and singular identification with the Lord, by putting on Jesus and His character as our armor – becoming a soldier in the Kingdom of God. We have rarely understood how to do this, so it is no wonder that so many of our battles end up in defeat.

Just imagine what our families, communities, nation and world would be like with the prevailing nature of God being expressed through His people instead of some religious dogma, including witchcraft.

God's nature is perfectly good, and we can be His expression of that goodness on the earth today. When we submit to His Kingdom, we know Him as the real benefactor of abundance. However, submitting to God's Kingdom is not always easy. We have to remember that everything that looks like God is not – it may actually be the devil.

Timothy told us that any form of godliness that denies the power of God to be transformed was just another religion.

That got my attention when I began to see that the power to live a whole life is our inheritance in the Kingdom of God. Look at the world around us and we see unprecedented immorality.

Timothy said that **"For men will be lovers of themselves, lovers of money, boasters, proud, blasphemers, disobedi-**

ent to parents, unthankful, unholy, unloving, unforgiving, slanderers, without self-control, brutal, despisers of good, traitors, headstrong, haughty, lovers of pleasure rather than lovers of God, having a form of godliness but denying its power. And from such people turn away"** (2 Timothy 3:2-5).

Without the power of God to transform our lives, the fruit of the Spirit is not available to give us an exchanged life. What is this "power" that Timothy talks about? I now understand that it is the compelling urge from within that causes us to act righteously.

The unrighteous traits that Satan tricks us with are what cause us to sin. The counter to sin is the righteousness of God in us. That is the fulfillment of His Kingdom. Instead of struggling with sinful acts, we should just submit to the Kingdom of God's Love in us and begin to abide in Him and He in us. When we do that, Jesus said that we could then ask anything that we would and it will be done (John 15:7).

The eyes of my understanding were truly being enlightened to the fact that religion without the indwelling love of God is self-defeating. The kingdom of Satan requires self-performance, but the Kingdom of God requires us to co-labor with Him.

Obviously, this liberating message of the Kingdom of God is the reason Jesus said that I was to seek it first and foremost. No doubt, I had to reject every religious spirit and form of godliness and begin to embrace God's Kingdom.

Chapter Eleven
The Gospel of the Kingdom

I knew that I was called to preach the gospel, but I was beginning to realize that maybe I did not know what the word "gospel" actually meant.

In Mark 16:15, Jesus said to them, **"Go into all the world and preach the gospel to every creature."**

What is the real meaning of the word gospel? Clearly, it means the good news of the teachings of Christ. What is the overarching teaching of Christ? <u>The Kingdom of God</u>! In Luke 4:43 Jesus clearly said that was why He was sent to earth.

In Matthew 4:23, it says that Jesus **"went about preaching the gospel of the Kingdom."** So to preach the gospel really means to preach the message of the Kingdom of God. In Matthew 24:14, Jesus said **"and this gospel of the Kingdom will be preached in the whole world as a witness to all the Nations, and then the end will come."**

Have we just ignored this all-important truth? If so, we have done an enormous disservice to the gospel message by only viewing it as a pathway to heaven.

God forgive us.

Discovering this kingdom emphasis as a huge part of the gospel was a process for me, and I know it will also be for others, but when we commit our mind to seeking the truth of the Kingdom, we will find it!

The gospel of salvation is the first and foremost step, but we must move beyond the elementary teachings about Christ to the vital teachings of God's Word where we find the power of the indwelling Kingdom of Love (Hebrews 6:1). It will give us victory over Satan's schemes and make us God's instruments for good in our homeland and around the world.

In the 7th century before Christ came to earth, the prophet Isaiah said in Chapter 9, verse 6 and 7, "**For unto us a child is born, unto us a son is given; and the <u>government</u> will be upon His shoulders; and His name will be called Wonderful, Counselor, The Mighty God, the Everlasting Father, the Prince of Peace. Of the increase of His <u>government</u> and peace there will be no end, Upon the throne of David, and over His <u>Kingdom</u>, <u>to order it</u> and to establish it with judgment and justice from that time forward even forever. The zeal of the Lord of Hosts will perform this**" (emphasis added).

It came to pass 2,000 plus years ago that that child Jesus came to earth, died, rose again and ascended into heaven with His father and became the King of kings. It was at that time that the Kingdom of God was established on earth.

The prophet stated that there is no end to His government, which is established to <u>bring order and justice</u> to the lives of those who believe and receive, and God's power will make this happen in us. If we fail to acknowledge a present and powerful Kingdom of God within us, through faith by grace, we will not accept and obey the government of God here and now.

God does not just grant us grace for our sake; He shares it through us to the world that He loves by motivating us to become a conduit of His provision. Matthew 10:8 says that "**Freely you have received, freely give**."

Grace that is not shared brings no life for us or for anyone else. It is like the Dead Sea, where water comes in, but does not go out. Nothing lives there, but when God's grace flows in our lives, it will flow out in abundance and thereby bless all of those within our sphere of influence. That is simply how the Kingdom of God operates.

It is a Kingdom that rules by grace that is established within us for the specific purpose of bringing order and blessing to our lives, here and now.

From the beginning, it was God's plan to send His son to Earth for the propitiation of our sins and to make us a new creature in Him. That is justification, which is the first step toward sharing God's life here on earth, but it is only the first step.

The next step is sanctification, which is the process of having our lives renewed to God's way of being righteous. We can accept the Kingdom of God or reject it and find ourselves submitting to the kingdom of darkness.

If we reject God's Kingdom, our lives will be ordered according to the scheme of the enemy, which is certainly not God's plan for us. It is a fact that we will submit to one kingdom or the other. There is no middle ground. Why would we not submit to the Kingdom of God when the choice is ours?

God has called us to a sanctified life, set apart for a divine purpose, but it can be fulfilled only by the divine nature of God. According to 2 Peter 1:4, it is our preordained destiny to be partakers of His divine nature, so that we can share it with others.

In fact, we already express certain character traits that we grow into that come from our parents, teachers, pastors and friends. It is imperative that we recognize that every good and righteous trait and act actually originates in the heart of God and is for the purpose of being shared through those who allow themselves to be a witness of His love.

We have to choose to submit to the work of the Holy Spirit in us in order to conform to the image of Christ.

Sanctification occurs when we embrace His character as our own, and thereby we produce fruits of righteousness and right works.

1 Thessalonians 4:3 (NIV) says, **"It is God's will that you**

should be sanctified." Certainly, we cannot sanctify ourselves. The only way for us to be sanctified is by allowing the Kingdom of God, within us, to identify with our spirit. Then God's character will empower us to live a fruitful life.

As a new creature in Christ, we are born again so that we may contain the love of God and have it operate through us by grace through faith.

How does that become effectual? God's love is supernatural, and we can't work it up – only receive it. Romans 5:17 says, "**For if by one man's offense death reigned through the one; much more those who receive abundance of grace and of the gift of righteousness will reign in life through the One, Jesus Christ.**"

If we want to reign in life, experience the joy of the Lord, the love of God, the righteousness of God, the peace that passes all understanding, and the abundant life on this earth, as well as life eternal, we must <u>receive</u> the abundance of His grace.

God has made it available for each of us to receive so that we can share it as we submit to His Kingdom. Again, we are reminded that "**Freely you have received, freely give**" (Matthew 10:8).

This is proof of the GOOD NEWS of the gospel. That good news will compel us to *become* the answer to the AIDS epidemic, the poverty, the crime, the unemployment and the hopelessness of our people.

The needs and the problems may look different around the world, but the solution is the same. "**But if the Spirit of Him who raised Jesus from the dead dwells in you, He who raised Christ from the dead will also give life to your mortal bodies through His Spirit who dwells in you**" (Romans 8:11). My orphans need more than man's medicine. They need the Kingdom of God to come to Zululand with power and provision, as it is in heaven.

Chapter Twelve
A KINGDOM OF LOVE

The consequences of getting it wrong about God's Kingdom are catastrophic.

We can see the evil result everywhere, in every home, village and nation. We truly are destroyed by a lack of knowledge and truth about the Kingdom.

We have allowed a great gulf to develop between the gospel of salvation and the Kingdom of God that has permitted life eternal with God but relegated us to hell on Earth.

How did this happen? We need the eyes of our understanding to be enlightened to truth about the Kingdom of God. Even though the Kingdom is in us and its efforts are felt all around us, we still have trouble identifying it for what it is.

A picture of what the Kingdom of God looks like was beginning to come into focus for me.

It is everything that Paul said in Phillippians 4:8-12 that we are to set our mind or affection on. He said, **"Finally, brethren, whatever things are true, whatever things are noble, whatever things are just, whatever things are pure, whatever things are lovely, whatever things are of good report, if there is any virtue and if there is anything praiseworthy – mediate on these things."**

When our mind focuses on these things and God's love is in us, it motivates us to action. *We actually become God's provision for each other, through our reasonable service*. Romans 12:1 (NIV) says that **"Therefore, I urge you, brothers and sisters, in view of God's mercy, to offer your bodies as**

a living sacrifice, holy and pleasing to God -- this is your true and proper worship."

I know of no better example of the Kingdom of God at work around us than the International Rotary Club with its commitment to the godly principle of *Service above Self.*

Rotary requires its members to ask four questions for a life of service. First, is it the truth? Second, is it fair to all concerned? Third, will it build good will and better friendships? And fourth, will it be beneficial to all concerned?

That should be an honest preface to every endeavor in life on Earth. These are the principles that flow out of the heart of God and produce life more abundantly. This is how we will see the Kingdom of God coming on earth as it is in heaven.

It will appear, not in words but in deeds. It will be motivated by the Spirit but manifest Itself in the flesh. It will cause us to seek to produce truth, justice and brotherly love, supported by mercy and grace. That must become our four-way test of the things we think, say or do. These are vital ingredients in the love of God and we, as his children, are authorized and empowered by Him to share them from His heart, through ours.

The Rotary Club, with its membership of over one million and clubs in two hundred countries, has just taken on the enormous task of immunizing every child in the world against polio and the five dreaded childhood diseases. Rotary has overseen its virtual eradication.

The Salvation Army, motivated by the love of God, is another great example, with its motto of *"Doing The Most Good."*

There are millions of other examples of the Kingdom of God at work, like prison ministry; strong families; community service; protecting the unborn; call to the mission field; caring for widows and orphans; and even simple things that we take for granted.

As Jesus said in Matthew 25:36-40 (NIV), **"I was na-**

ked and you clothed me, I was sick and you visited me, I was in prison and you came to me. Then the righteous will answer Him saying, Lord, when did we see you hungry and feed you, or thirsty and give you something to drink? When did we see you a stranger and invite you in or needing clothes and clothe you? When did we see you sick or in prison and go to visit you? The King will reply, Truly I say to you, whatever you did for one of the least of these brothers and sister, you did for me."

What the world calls charity is actually God's love in action through His children becoming His provision to others and His manna from heaven.

Why is this such a difficult concept to grasp?

The Kingdom of God is a Kingdom of Love! If God is love (and He is) and He lives in us (and He does), then so does His love. Why does God live in us? Do we think it is just because He needs some place to lay His head? He is everywhere (omnipresent).

The truth is that He is living in us in order to fulfill His scripture and plan, which is to have human beings submit to Him and share His love on earth as it is in heaven. His intention is for the love of God to be shed abroad through our hearts (Romans 5:5).

God's love always demands action and requires service above self-interest.

There are three Greek words for love. One is "eros," which stands for sexual or romantic love. This is the kind of love mostly known by the world. Then there is "philia," which generally refers to affection between friends. The word Philadelphia comes from this and is known as the "City of Brotherly Love."

Even though eros and philia have others as their focus, they are generally motivated by self-interest, self-gratification and self-protection. This is love that is designed to satisfy the desires of the one doing the loving. There may be an element of giving involved, but it is giving for the purpose of getting something in return.

The third Greek word for love is "agape." This love stands in stark contrast to the other two words. This word alone points to a completely self-sacrificing love, a love that lacks self-interest, self-gratification and self-preservation.

Agape love is motivated primarily by the interest and welfare of others. This is the Greek word most frequently used for the love of God. It means that we use our mind and our might for the benefit of others, without regard for ourselves. It is based not on our feelings, but a providential compulsion that derives from an inherent power to reproduce His love in us. That power equips us to comply with God's command to **"love one another"** (John 13:30).

The evidence of God's love is service to others in need.

The New Living Translation of the Bible says in Matthew 23:11 that **"The greatest among you will be your servant."** When we share God's love, the motivation behind it will be intense, almost tangible, and certainly palpable. It is like air that can't be seen or felt until is it provoked to movement. It then becomes a mighty force.

God's love is available to be shared through our physical bodies, simply by submission and divine direction. This Kingdom of love is resident in us, ready in season and out of season, to cause good to overcome evil.

It is sad that we have been hesitant to recognize the fact that _the plan of God is to inhabit His children now and make them instruments of righteousness, peace and joy_.

It is the Kingdom of God within us that is producing a compelling urge for us to do good by the power of the Holy Spirit, who motivates us to put feet to faith and voice to victory. We will find that we don't have a choice but to care for the sick, the hurting, the lonely, the homeless, the vulnerable and the widows and orphans.

It now makes perfect sense to me that God is not withholding His love and provision from us but is sharing it through those who acknowledge and respond to His Kingdom of Love. We, becoming the personification of His love, become the hope for this world now.

God's abundance becomes our provision when we give. We find that we are empowered by the joy of the Lord and revel in the Truth that **"It is more blessed to give than to receive"** (Act 20:35).

Unless we give by the inspiration of the Holy Spirit, we will give begrudgingly. Without acknowledging that every good thing comes from the Lord, we will take personal credit for the good that we do.

Chapter Thirteen
THE DIVIDED GOSPEL

I recently read an excellent exposé in a book titled *The Divided Gospel: The Consequences of Separating the Gospel from the Kingdom*, by Dr. Joseph Mattera.

The author identifies the effect of dismissing the Kingdom of God from our walk with God.

First, he says, "In the Kingdom, the focus is on manifesting God in the earth; in religion, the focus is on applying their traditions inside church buildings. Just the term kingdom implies both the king and his domain.

"Psalm 24:1 teaches us that the earth belongs to the Lord, and Psalm 22:28 says that His Kingdom rules over all nations, not just over the church. Consequently, we in His Kingdom (see Colossians 1:12-13) are called to manifest His rule in the whole earth, not just the church realm."

Second, "In the Kingdom an individual transforms from within; in religion the focus is on observing our rituals. Jesus taught us in Matthew 5:7, 23 that God requires truth in the inner man (see also Psalm 51:6). Hence, the Kingdom focuses on inside out transformation (see Luke 17:21) while religion focuses primarily on observing rituals during church services."

Third, "In the Kingdom, every sphere of life is integrated under King Jesus; in religion, the church stays out of the public square. The Kingdom of God integrates the rule of God with societal structure such as law, politics, economics, families, art, and business. In religion, politics and economics are unspiritual and should be left to the world."

Fourth, "In the Kingdom, the focus is on transforming the earth; in religion it is on perpetuating His traditions in the church."

Fifth, "In the Kingdom, culture is engaged; in religion, disengagement and escape from the earth are desired.

The nature of religion is that it wants to create its own enclave of safety from the unpredictable realties of the unredeemed world. Religion is mystical, not practical or spiritual. However, those trained in the Kingdom view every earthly challenge as an opportunity to be a problem solver and to bring Christ into culture."

It should be abundantly clear to all of us by now that the church, without the Kingdom message, is ineffective to influence the culture of a society or nation.

Many of us involved in the church seem ashamed of the gospel – at the least we are timid and easily intimidated. Why is that so, when Paul said that the gospel is the power of God unto salvation and we know that salvation means more than just going to heaven? The gospel without the Kingdom component is like a car without a motor – you are not going very far on your journey.

Like everything spiritual, the Kingdom of God seems foolish to a natural man because it can only be spiritually discerned and it is foolishness to a natural man (1 Cor. 2:14).

I confess that I had treated the Word of God about the Kingdom foolishly, shamefully and arrogantly.

Before I could move forward in my ministry, I had to seek God's forgiveness for doubting His ways. I now know that my commission is to go into all the world to disciple the nations, starting with mine, about the Kingdom of God.

As Jesus said in Matthew 28:18-20, we are to "**go therefore and make disciples of all the nations, baptizing them in the name of the Father and of the Son and of the Holy Spirit,**

**teaching them to observe all things that I have commanded
you...."**

Jesus is expecting us to teach the entirety of His Truth – not
just get saved, go to heaven and let the earth go to hell in a
hand basket.

Chapter Fourteen
AN AMERICAN PERSPECTIVE
By Robert L. Flournoy

I want to dedicate, with great appreciation, this part of the book to the Godly teachers, prophets and mentors who have led me to a place of renewal and revitalization of Christian life by God's perfect plan: His kingdom.

My mentors have been, and continue to be, the latter-day forerunners teaching the message of the Kingdom of God, like Simon Purvis, Jim Hodges, Miles Monroe, Chuck Pierce, Dr. Tony Evans, Dutch Sheets, E. Stanley Jones, Dudley Hall, Lance Wallnau, C. S. Lewis, Dr. Joseph Mattera and many others including Pat Francis with Kingdom Covenant Ministries in Toronto, that have dared to confront the religious dogma that wrote the obituary for the Kingdom of God.

I thank God for these courageous men and women. They all remind me of John the Baptist in the wilderness, declaring the Kingdom of God is at hand, except that my current colleagues are saying it is here now!

What does a Zulu warrior and a Texas cowboy have in common? Well, nothing until forty years ago, when Jeremiah became a born-again Christian in Africa and I became a born-again Christian in Texas the same year.

At that time, we became brothers, "from different mothers" as some say, but neither of us knew the other until twenty years later when we first met at my church in Texas.

Suddenly, our common denominator was Jesus Christ! It mattered not that he was black and I was white. He was raised in a mud hut and I in a structure in rural Texas that some call a mansion; I was raised on a large farm and cattle ranch and Jeremiah did not own even seven cows to pay for the dowry for his wife.

Jeremiah came from a very poor area of South Africa where witchcraft was and still is practiced. I was raised in a church, from infancy, but never knew the Lord personally until I was 38 years old. It seemed that Jeremiah and I were as different as night and day.

Most people would say that I was born with a silver spoon in my mouth, even though I don't remember it that way at all.

I, and my four siblings, worked harder on our farm and ranch than any slave ever would have. Fortunately, we were born to great parents, who valued the truth, gave us a good work ethic and a fine family above all else. Our folks appreciated Christianity, but did not know Christ personally until late in life.

In truth, we were Christians in name only, but were raised to be good and do good. In the world's eyes, we have done well and become successful. My oldest brother became an engineer, my next brother, a college professor, I, a lawyer, my youngest brother a banker and real estate developer and my wonderful sister a receptionist at a large paper mill.

I have been married to my amazing wife, Genie, for 56 years and have three wonderful children. The oldest is a business manager for a large engineering firm, my son is a lawyer, and my younger daughter is a business executive. I have six grandchildren and six great grandchildren.

By all accounts, I have lived a blessed and prosperous life. But Jeremiah, not so much.

How did Jeremiah and I become so much alike?

Neither of us paid much attention to the stark differences between us. He, like me, when we became a new person in Christ, began to submit to the love of God within us that transcended all of our differences.

We had a common, compelling desire to serve others. In pursuing my profession as a lawyer, the law became a mission field for me. Via an active role in our local Rotary Club where the motto is "Service above Self," I have been active in my community.

I have served for over fifty years on the Salvation Army Advisory Board where the motto of this organization is "Doing the Most Good."

And I have been serving faithfully in a spirit-filled church and submitting to a great teacher of God's word. Each of these give expression to who I had become in Christ.

Twenty years ago, when I first came to know Jeremiah, his commitment to serve the orphans and vulnerable children in his country agreed with my spirit and my desire to serve my country.

We were both excited about the hope that we had in the Lord but were completely frustrated and overwhelmed with the obvious lack of success that we were seeing.We were both questioning why we were not seeing the results God's word promised.

Personally, I began to rethink my theology. Like Jeremiah, I began to ask if there was something about the gospel that had escaped me.

Like the Galatians, had I been bewitched? As I thought back, I remembered that when I was born again, I was instantly convicted that the Bible was true and that I could trust every word.

I found that I had a voracious appetite for the scripture and studied it night and day for years. I knew the scripture in Romans 10:17 that said **"faith comes by hearing, and hearing by the word of God."**

I wanted to be a man of faith and thought I could get there by my own intellect and determination. My faith even made me feel good about my Christian commitment; however, that began to wear thin as my personal battles ended up in losses. Why was I losing more than winning?

I knew Satan was the author of everything bad – sickness, disease and poverty - and that he went around like a roaring lion seeking whom he may devour.

I knew he was a liar, but what I did not realize was that he was an amazing con artist. How could he pull one over on me as a Christian lawyer?

His was a shell game – he hid the ball from me for years. While I was concentrating on the physical things that he was promoting, I failed to see the mental game that he was playing with me. With all the skirmishes he had me involved in, he was manipulating my mind away from God's plan for victory over him.

One day, I was re-reading Galatians 2:20 in the King James version where Paul said, "**I am crucified with Christ: nevertheless I live; yet not I, but Christ liveth in me: and the life that I now live in the flesh, I live by the faith of the Son of God who loved me, and gave himself for me**."

In Galatians 2:21 he said, "**I do not frustrate the grace of God: for if righteousness come by the law, then Christ is dead in vain**."

I realized that I was very steeped in the law, but what was Paul saying? The next verse was Galatians 3:1, about the Galatians being foolishly bewitched. Surely, it was not talking about me.

Galatians 3:1-12 (KJV) said,

> **"O foolish Galatians, who hath bewitched you, that ye should not obey the truth, before whose eyes Jesus Christ hath been evidently set forth, crucified among you?"**
>
> **"This only would I learn of you, Received ye the**

Spirit by the works of the law, or by the hearing of faith?"

"Are ye so foolish? Having begun in the Spirit, are ye now made perfect by the flesh? "

"Have ye suffered so many things in vain? If it be yet in vain."

"He therefore that ministereth to you the Spirit, and worketh miracles among you, doeth he it by the works of the law, or by the hearing of faith?"

"Even as Abraham believed God, and it was accounted to him for righteousness."

"Know ye therefore that they which are of faith, the same are the children of Abraham."

"And the scripture, foreseeing that God would justify the heathen through faith, reached before the gospel unto Abraham, saying, In thee shall all nations be blessed. "

"So then they which be of faith are blessed with faithful Abraham."

"For as many as are of the works of the law are under the curse: for it is written, Cursed is every one that continueth not in all things which are written in the book of the law to do them."

"But that no man is justified by the law in the sight of God, it is evident: for, The just shall live by faith."

" And the law is not of faith: but, The man that doeth them shall live in them."

Like a bolt of lightning, I realized that I had been tricked by the enemy into believing that victory in this Christian life depended on how much faith I had. But in fact, it was how much of God's faith I had in me that I could identify with and appropriate.

The little preposition "of" in Galatians 2:20 changed my

Christian life.

Paul said, "**And the life that I now live in the flesh I live by the faith of the Son of God, who loved me, and gave himself for me.**"

Did it really say I could live my life by His faith? This was a shocking revelation! Obviously, I could not conjure up enough faith on my own to live in victory over the enemy. When I submitted to the faith that was already in me, in the person of Jesus Christ, along with His other character traits that flow out of love, it became clear that I could <u>live and move and have my being in Him</u> (Acts 17:28).

This revelation began to reshape my Christian life and belief system. "**Nevertheless I live, yet not I but Christ liveth in me.**" Paul said that he did not live by <u>faith in</u> the Son of God but by the <u>faith of</u> the Son of God.

What a relief! It really was Christ in me, the hope of glory. John 3:30 said it bluntly, "**He must increase, but I must decrease.**"

That did not stroke my ego, but it relieved all my anxiety about personally measuring up to God's standard. What a revelation! The King of kings was already in me, but on hold, until His power, authority, righteousness, peace and joy were revealed and accepted by me and then expressed through me.

With the knowledge of that reality, I discovered that God's character traits began to fight my battles. It was an incredible epiphany to me that the <u>Kingdom of God was God's plan for us all along</u>.

Even though I was listening to some incredible teachers and prophets, this revelation did not come by them but by the Spirit of God.

That was the same way that the reality that Jesus was the Son of God came to Simon Peter. Jesus told Peter that this knowledge of who Jesus was, was not revealed to him by flesh and blood but by the Spirit.

Revelation brings freedom because when you receive it by experience, you are no longer at the mercy of Satan's argument.

After that, I really tuned in to the teachings of the Holy Spirit, and the eyes of my understanding were enlightened.

One of the things that I was always concerned with was my country and its culture. It was obviously changing, and not for the better.

God literally showed me the ineffectiveness of the gospel of salvation alone to affect our societal norms.

As God divinely connected me with Jeremiah Mdlalose from the Zulu tribe in South Africa, I learned that he was also distressed about his culture.

The Zulu's problems seemed worse because their poverty and disease alone were staggering, in spite of the fact that they had a benevolent King and kingdom.

The Zulu nation had a form of government and power that appeared to be able to provide help, nourishment and peace to its people, but it had not done so for generations.

This was true even though many evangelists had come to South Africa and millions had accepted the Lord.

The people were not resistant to the gospel of salvation; in fact, they seemed to be much more receptive to Jesus than Americans are.

I attributed that to their need, but was it more? John 3:19 says "**the light has come into the world and men loved darkness rather than light because their deeds were evil.**"

Romans 1:25 (NIV) says "**Who exchanged the truth about God for a lie, and worshiped and served created things rather than the Creator?**" Was that where we all went wrong?

Certainly, that applied to the U.S. as much as to the Zulus, but I hated to admit it. Truth be known, the minds of the Americans are probably much darker than those of Africans toward the whole gospel.

In Revelation 3:17, it looks like John was talking about America when he said, "**Because you say, I am rich, I have become wealthy and have need of nothing; yet you do not know that you are wretched, pitiful, poor, blind and naked.**"

We mistakenly think that we are self-sufficient, but our pride holds us in bondage to more darkness than any African country. We readily call ourselves a Christian nation but have adopted a form of godliness that denies the power of God to have preeminence in our lives.

We are like the poem written by William Henley titled "Invictus":

> *Out of the night that covers me,*
> *Black as the Pit from pole to pole,*
> *I thank whatever gods may be*
> *For my unconquerable soul.*
>
> *In the fell clutch of circumstance*
> *I have not winced nor cried aloud.*
> *Under the bludgeonings of chance*
> *My head is bloody, but unbowed.*
>
> *Beyond this place of wrath and tears*
> *Looms but the Horror of the shade,*
> *And yet the menace of the years*
> *Finds, and shall find, me unafraid.*
>
> *It matters not how strait the gate,*
> *How charged with punishments the scroll.*
> *I am the master of my fate:*
> *I am the captain of my soul.*

(emphasis added)

Is that not Satan's best lie designed specifically for those that have worldly abundance, as we do in America? Exactly what did Jesus mean by abundant life?

I began to see that abundant life is not about what we have. It is not what we get. It is not about what we claim. Ultimately, life is about what we become by identifying with the Lord and determining to live knowing we are stewards of His blessings.

What have we received from the Lord? Himself! We get Him, together with His intangible character traits of love, joy, peace, long-suffering, patience, goodness, kindness, and mercy and we get the power to be those traits to our family, communities and nations.

The Kingdom of God is His divine nature adopted and expressed on this earth through His children.

It is **"righteousness and peace, and joy in the Holy Spirit"** (Romans 14:17). When our lives are submitted to the Creator, obedient to the Savior and taught and led by the Holy Spirit, then we will be quickened, committed and equipped to share the whole gospel to the world around us.

When we have enough of the intangible blessings of God to share directly from the heart of God to others, then we will truly have abundant life.

It is giving what has been given to us, just as Jesus said in John 14:27 (NIV), **"my peace I give you. I don't give to you as the world gives."**

The same is true with love, joy, peace and the fruit of the Spirit. The world cannot and will not give you His nature to share, because it is divine. The world will provide counterfeit character that exalts man, but it does not produce the life that already resides in the born-again Christian through a relationship with Jesus Christ.

The enemy tricks Americans with a feeling of self-sufficiency but uses hopelessness and the lack of self-worth to fool so many Zulus and many others in the third-world countries.

The end result is the same: we all turn our attention to something or someone else instead of God's real plan for us, which is an exchanged life by the power and persuasion of the Holy Spirit.

The great British writer, scholar and biblical apologist (defender of the word of God), C. S. Lewis wrote a book called The Screwtape Letters, where the devil, Screwtape, explains to his nephew and chief minion Wormwood how to deceive Christians. It is fiction, but its truth is absolutely staggering.

Please read it! It clearly reveals Satan's scheme to deceive and destroy man's destiny in the Lord. It is Satan's plan to stop the proliferation of the message of the Kingdom of God, and because Satan hates God, he will use any lie and deception to accomplish that plan.

Satan uses witchcraft in its purist form but not necessarily its most obvious. The same scheme does not work for everyone, but don't be complacent, for he has thousands of tactics that he will employ when the opportunity permits. Just listen to Screwtape's examples. You will be able to identify with some of them.

America has moved beyond being self-sufficient to now being self-absorbed, obsessed and in reality self-possessed.

We leave no room for God except as a Savior for eternity. Even then, most self-absorbed people believe that if there is a life hereafter and if there is a God, they will be okay because they are pretty good people and a good God would not reject them.

With many, they become their own deity and make an idol of their works.

Then there are those that think they are beyond salvation. They are the rejected by society, the abandoned, the victims, and they feel they are too worthless even for God to save. They cannot see that they are only victims to the lies of the devil.

And, because spiritual things are spiritually discerned, the message of God's plan and goodness escapes them. They are much like the religious leaders that Jesus dealt with that put Him on the cross.

American society has submitted to Satan's way for so long that it has moved from sin to iniquity, which is the promotion of ungodly ideas and ways.

We are already promoting: murder of babies for convenience, socialist government to create greater dependence on the state, irresponsible spending, destruction of the work ethic, games of chance, homosexuality, gender dysphoria, transsexualism, same-sex "marriage," situational ethics, disrespect for law and law enforcement, abuse of drugs, worship of beauty, decadence and a thousand other "if it feels good do it" ungodly ideas.

Self-interest becomes its own religion, denying the authority and power of God to be and provide His abundant life for us. When man is left to his own devices, he will serve his own lust of the eyes, lust of the flesh and the pride of life (1 John 2:16), leaving no room for God.

In America, many churches are self-absorbed with serving their self-absorbed members. They can justify their existence by promoting good works while still declaring the inerrancy of the Word of God. They can leave God out of the equation and just refer to the "good book" when they want to, and still promote man as the center of the universe. The fact is, many who identify themselves as Christians rarely read the scriptures or pray.

How did America get to the place where we should have to apologize to Sodom and Gomorrah?

We have done exactly what they did and submitted to the witchcraft that tickles our ears.

Satan has to simply twist the words to make them spiritually or politically pleasing for the times. He can make the Ten Commandments the ten suggestions or begin to call good evil and evil good.

He does not have to deny there is a Kingdom of God, just suggest that it is not for here or now. What begins as a suggestion and then is dwelled upon as an idea will become a dogma simply because the unreformed and unrenewed mind already opposes God.

Satan has a specific excuse designed for each of us to deny God and particularly to deny His Kingdom. Satan knows that he can create a reprobate mind in us (Romans 1:28) whether in America, or Zululand or anywhere else.

He will encourage man to create his own religion or adopt ancestor worship, voodooism, Islam, or Hinduism (that has millions of gods). The end result is the same, rejection of the Creator, the one true God.

The Kingdom of God is available only to a born-again person, for only then can the natural body contain the Spirit of God.

Satan understands that and does not want it to happen; but if it does, the liar can contain the effect of that transformed body on the culture by controlling the mind of man, which still has to be renewed to the truth (Romans 12:2).

Satan knows that the Kingdom of God, in full effect in man, will spell defeat for him and victory for mankind on this earth now. When the King is in charge, Satan's lies will be exposed and rejected, and his plan to exalt himself above the throne of God will be utterly destroyed.

When we submit ourselves to God and His Kingdom, the devil will flee. Otherwise, as the saying goes, "you give him an inch and he will become a ruler."

And so we have, and he is, by making us even more resistant to the message of the Kingdom in America than in Zululand.

The good news is that when the kingdom of America and the kingdom of the Zulu Nation begin to submit to the truth of God's Kingdom, then **"The kingdoms of this world have become the kingdoms of our Lord and His Christ; and He shall reign forever and ever"** (Revelation 11:15).

I now know what Romans 8:19 means when it says that the creation is waiting and the world is groaning for the manifestation of the sons of God on the earth.

Most historical kings maintained their kingdoms by force and demanded absolute allegiance to the king.

And so it was with the United Kingdom and the Zulu Kingdom. Now, most kings are figureheads, or they are kings with another title such as President, Supreme Leader, Ayatollah, Emperor, or Monarch.

Nonetheless, they rule dictatorially unless they accept and adopt the Christian concept of democracy, where the people decide who their leaders will be.

Eventually, however, even that form of government will devolve into a socialist state where a strong government controls and the people become subjected again, always with despotic leadership.

That is not so with the Kingdom of God, for it is maintained by consent of the governed. Its membership is offered, not conscripted. There are no weapons of war that maintain allegiance; there is only the power of love.

This is diametrically opposed to what we have imagined a kingdom to be.

There is only one government that can and will produce real and lasting freedom and abundant life, and that is the government of God, and its leader is the King of kings – Jesus Christ.

The realm of His rule is in the hearts of man, and the form of His rule derives from love, which naturally produces peace, joy, long-suffering, patience, kindness, goodness and mercy.

It requires only the consent of man to an all-powerful and loving Ruler, and then He does the work in and through us that affects our families, communities and nation. This is the one time we can be sure that if it seems too good to be true, it is still true.

Without question, the only way we can live life on this earth in peace, harmony and prosperity is when "the love of God is shed abroad in our hearts" (Romans 5:5). Paul described what that love is like in 1 Corinthians 13:1-10 (MSG):

> **The Way of Love**
> **[1]If I speak with human eloquence and angelic ecstasy but don't love, I'm nothing but the creaking of a rusty gate. [2]If I speak God's Word with power, revealing all his mysteries and making everything plain as day, and if I have faith that says to a mountain, "Jump," and it jumps, but I don't love, I'm nothing.**
>
> **[3-7]If I give everything I own to the poor and even go to the stake to be burned as a martyr, but I don't love, I've gotten nowhere. So, no matter what I say, what I believe, and what I do, I'm bankrupt without love.**
>> **Love never gives up.**
>> **Love cares more for others than for self.**
>> **Love doesn't want what it doesn't have.**
>> **Love doesn't strut,**
>> **Doesn't have a swelled head,**
>> **Doesn't force itself on others,**
>> **Isn't always "me first,"**
>> **Doesn't fly off the handle,**
>> **Doesn't keep score of the sins of others,**
>> **Doesn't revel when others grovel,**
>> **Takes pleasure in the flowering of truth,**
>> **Puts up with anything,**
>> **Trusts God always,**

Always looks for the best,
Never looks back,
But keeps going to the end.
[8-10]Love never dies. Inspired speech will be over some day; praying in tongues will end; understanding will reach its limit. We know only a portion of the truth, and what we say about God is always incomplete. But when the Complete arrives, our incompletes will be canceled.

The power of love can make all things new. Again, C.S. Lewis, in his book *Mere Christianity,* said it so well: "God became man to turn creatures into sons, not simply to produce better men of the old kind but to produce a new kind of man. It is not like teaching a horse to jump better and better but like turning a horse into a winged creature."

The Kingdom of God is love personified. In Lewis' last sermon he quoted William Law as saying, "If you have not chosen the Kingdom of God, it will make no difference in the end what you have chosen instead."

Lewis went on to say, "Those are hard words to take, but it will really make no difference whether it was women or patriotism, cocaine or art, or whiskey or a seat in the Cabinet, money or science? Well, surely no difference that matters. We shall have missed the end for which we are formed and rejected the only thing that satisfies."

"Does it matter to a dying man in the desert by which choice of route he missed the only well?"

Where do we go from here? **Believe God** (John 6:29); **seek His Kingdom** (Matthew 6:33); **stand against the wiles of the devil** (Ephesians 6:11); **embrace His divine nature** (2 Peter 1:4); **receive God's impartation of authority and the keys to the Kingdom** (Matthew 16:19); **accept God's promise that** those who receive the abundance of grace and the gift of righteousness shall reign in life by Christ Jesus (Romans 5:17); give thanks (I Thessalonians 5:18); and then take responsibility for our ultimate commission, which is to begin to disciple the nations about, by and through, the Kingdom of God (Matthew 28:19).

EPILOGUE

Boiling it all down, the Zulu warrior and the Texas cowboy are learning and experiencing "the rest of the story," as the former American radio broadcaster Paul Harvey would say.

The Kingdom of God is the greatest part of the greatest story ever told.

Our Creator has made us to be conformed to His own image and that image is nothing more and nothing less than love, for "**God is love**" (1 John 4:7-9).

"**Beloved, let us love one another, for love is of God; and everyone who loves is born of God and knows God.**"

Love must become our life, and it will become our life style.

It is God's perfect plan for us individually and collectively to submit to the Kingdom of God within us and to allow His love to be shed abroad in our hearts.

That love will accomplish His will because of the power of God that is inherent in it, and it will provoke and lead us in paths of righteousness and service to others.

When God's born-again people find their God-ordained and predestined purpose on this Earth, through His Kingdom, help, health, hope, peace and prosperity will be in abundance, with every need being met.

God's love, shared through the hearts of an army of believers, is exactly what these orphans and all mankind need. His love becomes our weapon of war against poverty, conflict, corruption and immorality. It is able to transform a miserable existence into a beautiful, healthy, prosperous and dynamic force for good. Whenever we identify and embrace His Kingdom, we will find our purpose and begin to live life to its full-est, here and now. We will really know, experience and share the message of the Kingdom of God, which is the Good News of the Gospel.

Since God's plan for us depends upon God's love in us, that plan is available to <u>every</u> born-again Christian, and nothing can prevent its effectual working in us except our own igno-rance and disobedience.

Like Paul, we must be fully "**persuaded that neither death nor life, nor angels nor principalities, nor powers, nor things present nor things to come, nor height, nor depth, nor any other created thing, shall be able to separate us from the love of God, which is in Christ Jesus our Lord**" (Romans 8: 38-39).

Selah (Pause and think about this).

REVIEWS

Finally, someone is asking the right questions and testifying to the Truth about the Kingdom of God. Jeremiah's book should become the definitive treatise on rediscovering the Gospel's actual ordained application to life on earth rather than just life after death.

Simon Purvis
Word of Life Teaching Center
Lufkin, Texas

A friendship between an African and a Texan has produced one of the most dynamic books I have ever read. In this well written volume, the reader will discover many insights about the power clashes between the Kingdom of God and the power of darkness which are battling for the inheritance of the earth! You will be inspired and instructed and, most of all, you will be strengthened in your faith and service to King Jesus!

Jim Hodges
President and Founder
Federation of Ministers and Churches
Duncanville, Texas

Jeremiah's personal story and his insights into scripture are extraordinary. One might say that the only explanation for his amazing life and ministry is God's intervention. How could the son of a penniless Zulu ever hope to study in the United States and one day become an advocate for widows and orphans among his own people? I have known pastor Jeremiah for more than twenty years. I have heard him preach countless times and I have prayed with him. This book will inspire and challenge you because it was written by one with a heart and zeal for the Kingdom of God.

Michael D. Thomas, Ph.d.
Department of Modern Languages and Cultures
Honors College
Baylor University
Waco, Texas

Personal Notes

Personal Notes

_____

_____

_____

_____

_____

_____

_____

_____

_____

_____

_____

_____

_____

_____

Personal Notes

CPSIA information can be obtained
at www.ICGtesting.com
Printed in the USA
FSHW022314080519

9 780982 747957